PRAYING
the Holy
Scriptures

M. Basil Pennington, OCSO

PARACLETE PRESS
BREWSTER, MASSACHUSETTS

Praying the Holy Scriptures

2012 First Printing

Copyright © 2012 by St. Joseph's Abbey

ISBN: 978-1-61261-141-9 (Pack of Five)

The Library of Congress has catalogued the original book *Seeking His Mind: Forty Meetings with Christ*, from which this book is excerpted, as follows:

Pennington, M. Basil.
  Seeking His mind : 40 meetings with Christ / M. Basil Pennington.
    p. cm.
  ISBN 1-55725-308-0
  1 Jesus Christ—Meditations. I. Title.
BT306.43.P46 2002
242–dc21   2002100836
10 9 8 7 6 5 4 3 2 1

Published by Paraclete Press
Brewster, Massachusetts
www.paracletepress.com

Printed in the United States of America

Let the same mind be in you that was in
    Christ Jesus,
who, though he was in the form of God,
did not regard equality with God
as something to be exploited,
but emptied himself,
taking the form of a slave,
being born in human likeness.
And being found in human form,
he humbled himself
and became obedient to the point of death—
even death on a cross.

PHILIPPIANS 2:5–8

CONTENTS

A Christian Way to Transformation

Anyone who has been in love or who has had a close friendship will understand. I look forward every day to meeting the Lord in lectio. It is a time of intimacy, of heart to heart. We know the Lord is truly present in his inspired Word. Here I find him and eagerly wait to hear what he has to say to me. "Speak, Lord, your servant, your friend, your disciple, wants to hear." I never know what he is going to say. And oftentimes he does quite surprise me.

His gift is always a word of life, whether it is an immediate flash of light or a word I must carry with me for a time before it shines forth. This is the excitement of lectio. Through his word, I see things differently.

What is lectio?

Lectio, or lectio divina, is for the Christian a whole process summed up in four words: lectio, meditatio, oratio, and contemplatio. This process is geared towards a transformation of consciousness and life. "Let this mind be in you which was in Christ Jesus," says St. Paul. Our aim is to have the "mind of Christ," the *nous Christou*, to see things, to evaluate all things, to respond to reality in the way Christ our Lord and Master does—to see things as God sees them.

Let me develop this process.

Lectio does not simply mean "reading," even though that is its literal translation. We are speaking of a way of Christian spirituality that prevailed through many centuries when the vast number of Christian people could not read. I think lectio here can most properly be understood as meaning "to receive the revelation." We Christians, sharing this in part with our Jewish brothers and sisters, are sons and daughters of the Book. And God, who of old spoke first through the creation and then through the prophets, has in these last days spoken to us through his incarnate Son, our Lord Jesus. Lectio most properly resides in hearing the word of God.

In an earlier period, memories seem to have been sharper, or were used more. It was not uncommon for an average Christian to know by heart extensive passages of Scripture, perhaps even the whole of the Gospels and the Psalter. Men like the venerable Abbot Bernard of Clairvaux were reputed to know the whole Bible. These Christians, then, always carried the Scriptures with them and at any moment, drawing on memory, could hear the word of God.

The word of God revealed itself in other ways, too: in the shared faith of sisters and brothers. The Reformers laid great stress on the sermon, as did the Fathers, whose great sermons have come down to us. Faith is also shared in less formal settings, in small groups, or in the one-to-one encounter. Out of our experience of the word, enlightened by the Holy Spirit, we speak the word to one another.

The word can be heard through other media. Music, certainly. Powerful hymns repeat themselves insistently within us: "Amazing grace, how sweet the sound." Art, the frescoes, icons, and stained glass windows. The earliest Christian assemblies, gathering in homes and catacombs, adorned the walls of their meeting places with scenes from the Scriptures. Our eastern Christian sisters and brothers find a real presence in icons and enshrine them in their homes as well as in their churches. The whole of the Scriptures is depicted in the windows of the great medieval cathedrals, such as Chartres.

The Master Artist does not cease to reveal himself in his masterpiece, the creation. As St. Paul reminded the Romans, for the mind that would see, God has always been there to be seen. Bernard of Clairvaux is noted for the saying that has been rendered into rather trite English: "I have found God more in the trees and the brooks than in the books." Above all does God reveal himself in that which is greatest in all creation, his own image and likeness, the graced person. In others, and in our very selves, we can experience the goodness and love of God, God himself, if we would but be still and know that he is God.

In colloquial English we have the expression: "I read you." It implies that I fully get what someone is trying to convey to me. This is perhaps a good translation of lectio, to "read" in this sense: to get God and all he is saying in all the many ways he is speaking.

An Ancient Method

Lectio, then, does not necessarily mean sitting with a book. It can mean looking at a work of art, standing before an icon, listening to a friend's word of faith, or taking a walk, letting the beauty of the creation, which often lies beneath layers of sin's ugliness, speak to us. But for most of us, the most constant, chosen, and privileged hearing of the word will be when we sit daily with the Book, the inspired Word of God.

ONE

Three Steps to Daily Lectio

I WOULD LIKE AT THIS POINT TO TAKE A few minutes to share a very simple and practical way of doing our daily lectio. This simple method comes from the age-old practice of the monks and nuns as expressed in their customaries. I will present it in three points, for that seems a very traditional way to do it and aids memory.

1. **Come into Presence and call upon the Spirit.** The old monastic usages say that when a nun or monk is going to do lectio, she or he takes the Holy Scriptures, kneels, prays to the Holy Spirit, reads the first sentence, and then reverently kisses the sacred text. We have two elements here: coming into the presence of God dwelling in his inspired word, and asking his Holy Spirit to help us in our lectio.

If one enters the abbatial church at St. Joseph's Abbey (and this is not the only place one will find this), one will always find two lamps burning: one burns before the tabernacle, proclaiming the real presence of Christ in the Eucharist; the other burns before the sacred text enthroned in the middle of the choir, proclaiming a real presence of Christ the

Word in his Scriptures. The Word abides in the Bible ever ready to speak to us. Our Bibles should never be just put on the shelf with other books or left lying haphazardly on our desks. They should be enshrined in our homes and offices, proclaiming a real presence. When we come to our lectio, we take the book with great reverence and respond to that presence. Acknowledging the Lord's presence in his word, we are ready to listen.

And we call upon the Holy Spirit to help us to hear. In his last discourse at the supper on the night before he died, Jesus promised to send the Holy Spirit, the Paraclete, to abide with us, to teach us, and to call to mind all he had taught us. It is the Holy Spirit who inspired the writers of the Sacred Text. This same Holy Spirit dwells in us. We ask him now to make the message, the word of life in the text he inspired, come alive now for us and truly speak to us.

2. **Listen for ten or fifteen minutes.** One can choose any length of time that satisfies, but ten or fifteen minutes can be enough for the Lord to give us a word of life. We are busy people; it is difficult to make time—we don't find it, we have to make it, for all the things we want to do each day. But who cannot make ten minutes for something if he or she really wants to? The point here is that we listen for a period of time. The nun or monk will usually sit at her or his lectio until the next bell rings. You do not usually have bells to summon you from one thing to another, but you can set a time. What

we want to avoid is setting a goal for ourselves to read a page, a chapter, or a section. We are so programmed to speed reading, to getting things done, that if we set ourselves to read a certain amount, we will be pushed to get it done. We do not want that. We want to be able to listen to the Word freely. If he speaks to us in the first or second sentence, we want to be free to abide there and let that word of life resound in us, going on only when we feel we have responded to him as fully as we wish for the moment. If in our lectio time we hear only a sentence or two—fine! The important thing is to hear the Word, to let him speak to us. That is why in the second point we say "we listen," not "we read."

3. **At the end of the time, "take a word" and thank the Lord.** In doing this, we thank the Lord. It is a wonderful thing that at any time we wish we can get God almighty, our Lord God, to sit down and speak to us. We often have to make appointments and do a lot of waiting to get his representatives to give us some time and attention. But not so with the Lord. This moment of thanksgiving emphasizes again the real presence. God has truly made himself available to us and spoken to us through his word; we thank him.

We "take a word." Word here does not mean necessarily a single word; it can connote a sentence or a phrase. It means a meaningful message summed up in one or a few words. In the earliest Christian times, devout women and men would go to a spiritual mother or father and ask them for a "word of life," a brief directive that would guide them in the way of Christian holiness.

A man asked Amma Syncletica, "Give me a word." The old woman said, "If you observe the following you can be saved: Be joyful at all times, pray without ceasing, and give thanks in all things."

Abba Pambo asked Abba Anthony, "What ought I to do?" and the old man said to him, "Do not trust in your own righteousness, do not worry about the past, control your tongue and your stomach."

Brother Bruno asked Father Basil, "Give me a word of life, Father." "Say, 'I am God's son,' and live accordingly," was the reply.

As we listen to the Lord in our daily lectio, we ask him for a word of life. Some days he does very clearly speak to us. Some word or phrase of the text seems virtually to shout at us. He speaks and we hear him.

Many of us have had our Taboric or Damascus moments. Such words change our lives and remain always with us, never far from our consciousness. Other times his word is not so dramatically spoken. And there are days when he does not seem to speak at all. We read on and on, listening, but nothing strikes home. On such days we have to take a word and carry it with us. Often, later in the day, it will speak, if not for us, for another.

Guerric of Igny, a twelfth-century Cistercian monk, in an Easter sermon comments on the Gospel

scene where the three women who failed to find
Christ at the empty tomb suddenly encounter him
on the garden path. Guerric says to his brothers:
"You know how it is, brothers. Some days we go
to our lectio and the Lord is not there; we go
to the tomb of the altar and he is not there;
and then, as we are going out to work, lo, halfway
down the garden path we meet him." The word
we have taken may suddenly come alive for us
as we are conversing with someone else, or
drying the dishes, or puzzling over something
altogether different.

TWO
Waiting on the Lord

As we learn to pray with Holy Scripture, we practice not only lectio but also meditatio, oratio, and finally, contemplatio. This really is not complicated.

FROM LECTIO TO CONTEMPLATIO

If each day a word of the Lord can truly come alive for us and can form our mind and heart, we will come indeed to live by faith as just persons; we will have that mind of Christ. This is precisely the aim of meditatio.

Again, I hesitate to translate the word *meditatio* directly. Meditation has come to have various meanings for us. Perhaps the most prevalent meaning is that given to it in modern English Hindu terminology. This may be a commentary on how poorly we Christians have made our own heritage present and available. We have all heard of transcendental meditation. In this Eastern sense, meditation means a certain emptiness, openness, presence to the absolute, to the nothingness, the beyond, and the practices that seek to take us into such a state. In more recent Christian usage, meditation has meant searching out the facts and mysteries of revelation to understand them better, to be moved to respond to them, and to bring their influence into our lives. It has been largely a rational exercise ordered toward affective and effective response. Meditatio in the earlier Christian tradition has a meaning that perhaps can be seen as lying somewhere between these two modern meanings.

Meditatio in this tradition meant repeating the word one had received from lectio—whatever form it took: reading, the faith sharing of a father, the proclamation in the assembly—repeating it perhaps on the lips, at least in the mind, until it formed the heart; until, as the Fathers sometimes expressed it, the mind descended into the heart. On a couple of occasions, St. Luke in his Gospel tells us that Mary pondered or weighed certain events in her heart.

He is pointing toward meditation of this sort. The word is allowed simply to be there, letting its weight, its own gravity, press upon us till it gives form to the attitude of our heart. The result is oratio.

Again, I hesitate to translate oratio simply as "prayer." Too easily do we think of prayer as asking God for something or conversing with him or saying prayers. All of that is indeed prayer and can be good prayer. But here, when the Fathers speak of oratio, they mean something different; they mean something very powerful and urgent: fiery prayer, darts of fire that shoot out from the heart into the very heart of God. As the psalmist sings: "In my meditation fire burst forth." It is prayer in the Holy Spirit. It is brief. It is total. When the word finally penetrates and touches the core of our being, it calls forth this powerful response, whether it be a cry of praise, love, petition, thanksgiving, reparation, or some mixture of all of these, according to the particular word and circumstances.

This is pure prayer. For a moment it takes us beyond ourselves. It calls forth from us a response so complete that for the moment we are wholly in the response. For a moment we leave behind all consideration of ourselves, all the usual self-reflection or self-awareness; we are totally in the response. It is a moment when we fulfill the first and greatest commandment: We love the Lord our God with our whole mind, our whole heart, our whole soul, and all our strength.

Such moments are very special, very wonderful. We want them to return, we want them to go on and on; in a word, we want contemplatio. For this is what contemplation means: the word has so formed us and called us forth, that we abide in total response. Our whole being is a yes to God as he has revealed himself to us. We are, as the Book of Revelation says of Christ, an Amen to the Father.

This transformation of consciousness we cannot bring about by ourselves. It is beyond us. We can prepare ourselves for it, seek it, and dispose ourselves for it. We can actively prepare for it by

seeking to let go of the things that have a hold on
us and keep us from being free to be a complete
yes to God. This is the role of self-denial or
mortification. Our Master spoke of taking up
our cross daily, denying ourselves, dying to self:
"Unless the grain of wheat fall in the ground
and die. . . " We have to be willing to let go of
self, that constant watching of self, that wanting
to be right, to be always correct; and turn both
eyes, our whole attention, on God, so that we
can truly and freely hear his word. We seek this
transformation by listening to the word of God
with openness, letting it in and letting it reform
us, through lectio and meditatio. We can dispose
ourselves for transformation by making spaces for
God to come in and reveal himself in himself, and
in that revealing, transform us. "Be still," he says,
"and know that I am God."

God made us. He knows us through and
through, and he respects us as no one else does.
He knows the greatest thing he has given us is our
freedom, because therein lies our power to love, to
be like him who is love. He respects our freedom.
He will never force his way into our lives: "Behold,
I stand at the door and knock. And if one opens, I
will come in. . . ." We first open the door by lectio;
we further open it by silent attentive presence.
When the received word has formed our hearts
and, through the passing experiences of fiery prayer,

creates in us a desire for an abiding transformation, an abiding state of prayer in presence, we begin to want to cultivate interior quietness, silence, and space in expectant longing. The Fathers have passed down to us a method for cultivating this prayer of the heart. Centering prayer is a modern presentation of this traditional method. But any method is only dispositive. It is a concrete way of asking, of seeking. Contemplative prayer remains a gift. We dispose ourselves in a stillness that expresses an intent, loving longing. And then he comes, when he wills. Much of our time may be spent in expectant, silent waiting. We may murmur again and again his name, our word of love and longing. But we can only wait till he comes and with his touch draws us forth beyond ourselves into the knowledge, the experiential knowledge, of himself, which transforms our consciousness.

According as he gives, this transformed state of consciousness becomes more abiding, until by his grace and mercy it quietly prevails even in the midst of our many activities. In this state of consciousness we come to see things as he sees them, value them as he values them. We seek to become full collaborators with him in bringing about by love and service the redeeming transformation of the world. I will not develop here at length the effects of this lived transformation of consciousness, but I think one can readily surmise how it will affect our relationships with others, and with the rest of creation. It certainly provides the base for global community and ecological reverence.

Most striking about this is its simplicity. We have but to open ourselves to the revealing and all-powerful word of God and he will do the rest. It is simple, but not easy. For such openness implies making time and space to hear. Making time is difficult enough in our busy lives. Making space in our cluttered hearts is more difficult, for if each day we take the next step in faithfulness to his revealing word, in the end we will have to give up everything. But this is only in order to have the space to find everything, with him and in him, in all its potential fullness and magnificence, no longer bound by the confines of our limitations. In this way we come to live the first great commandment to love the Lord our God with our whole mind, our whole heart, our whole soul, and our whole strength; and the second, which is like unto it, to love our neighbors and the whole creation as we love ourselves in that first great love. It is to be wholly in "The Way," who is the way to the Father in the Holy Spirit of Love.

Using Our Imaginations

As WE LISTEN TO THE LORD IN THE HOLY
Scriptures our imagination comes into play. There
is a time and place to use this wonderful faculty
God has given us.

If we may speak so anthropomorphically, just
think of the imagination God has exercised in
creating this wonderful world of ours. How he must
have delighted in making all the different flowers
and trees with their varied colors, especially in the
fall, not to speak of the ever-changing clouds. Think
of the animal kingdom, the tropical fish beyond
counting, and you and me and all our sisters and
brothers—what variety, what imagination!

Perhaps God's most imaginative act was when
he decided himself to become a Jewish carpenter,
born of a virgin, and to die on a cross to give an
ultimate sign of love. And what imagination we see
in Jesus! Think of his many stories and parables:
the workers in the vineyard, the prodigal son, the
good shepherd, the searching housewife, and so
many more. Everyday things became fabric for his
canvas—"Which of you when your child asks for
an egg would give the child a stone?" And there are
his many "signs." Did not his imagination reach a

summit when he undertook to change bread into
his very self and give us to eat? What a sign of self-
giving and nurturing love!

His church, the one he founded, continued
to use imagination in surrounding this eucharistic
sign with a rich, symbolic liturgy taking many
forms, ever adapting itself to different peoples
and changing times. Imagination is behind the
whole sacramental system and the never-ending
challenge to find the language (a collection of
creative symbols) to express the inexpressible.

The Scriptures resort to imaginative stories and
myths to express what is too big for our logical
concepts. Letting the Scriptures come alive in our
imagination, we have the challenge to hear what they
are saying to us today and to share that with others.

Yes, it is not only for the Church as a whole, the
Church as the divinely constituted teacher, but also
for each one of us to use our imagination to enter
into what is beyond and to share what we receive.

My nephew claims to have watched *The Lion King*
twenty-three times with his little daughter. Little
ones never tire of images and flights of imagination.
Jesus said, "Unless you become as little ones, you
will not enter the kingdom of heaven." We need
to let the Holy Scriptures fill our imaginations and
give us the images that will stir our emotions and
motivate our wills to seek wholeheartedly what
is beyond, but what alone can satisfy our hearts,
which are made for the divine.

FOUR

Ten Short Examples

AND NOW, LET ME OFFER YOU TEN BRIEF
examples of what the Lord has given to me during
my daily times of praying with the Holy Scriptures.
May they encourage you to spend time daily with
him, too. Each of these passages from the Gospels
is a rich place to start!

MARY BRINGS JESUS

LUKE 1:39–45

In those days Mary set out and went with haste to a Judean town in the hill country, where she entered the house of Zechariah and greeted Elizabeth. When Elizabeth heard Mary's greeting, the child leaped in her womb. And Elizabeth was filled with the Holy Spirit and exclaimed with a loud cry, "Blessed are you among women, and blessed is the fruit of your womb. And why has this happened to me, that the mother of my Lord comes to me? For as soon as I heard the sound of your greeting, the child in my womb leaped for joy. And blessed is she who believed that there would be a fulfillment of what was spoken to her by the Lord."

For me one of the inspiring, courageous stories of the Bible is the story of the event that we call the Visitation. A beautiful young woman who has just become pregnant, who has just been told she is the mother of God, forgetting herself, heads off across an alien land to bring succor to an aged cousin.

I daresay most women, on becoming pregnant, especially with their first pregnancy, begin to center a bit more on self. Should the mother of God be running off to serve the mother of her son's forerunner? Should it not be just the opposite? At least, should she not be allowed to rest at home in safety, surrounded by loving care? And how was Joseph going to handle this? Shouldn't she stay and work this out with him before her condition becomes obvious? And what of the dangers of the journey? The hostility of the Samaritans was proverbial, and she would be traveling alone.

The angel didn't tell Mary she should go. The divine messenger only announced her cousin's condition. Mary was certainly in a unique position to accompany her elderly cousin in her extraordinary pregnancy, and no doubt a part of Mary longed to have a female friend with whom she could share her own growing experience. But her compassionate heart was for her cousin. So off she went.

Only on seven occasions do the Gospels recount a word from the mouth of the mother of God. But on this occasion we are not even told what the words were. Perhaps it is to leave the space open, for when Mary comes to us her presence is expressed in so many different ways. In any case, cousin Elizabeth clues us in: "As soon as I heard the sound of your greeting . . ." The simple experience of Mary's presence was all that mattered.

Then what? The child in Elizabeth's womb leaped for joy, being filled with the Holy Spirit. Elizabeth herself was filled with a discerning spirit, calling Mary "the mother of my Lord"—she recognized her at once.

I believe this particular incident is recounted in the opening pages of the Gospel, as our Savior begins his salvific mission, to invite us to be aware of Mary's oft-hidden but very important role in the story of salvation.

It is she who brings Christ, to sanctify, to fill with leaping joy, to enlighten, to console and comfort and strengthen. This is Mary's mission in history and in the life of each one of us.

It is Mary who brings Christ to us. And she brings us a faith that can withstand even the test of a Holy Saturday, when the faith of all others seems to fail. When we sense her presence, we gain courage, comfort, hope, and joy and direction.

We do not know how Elizabeth, who had concealed herself during this time of wondrous pregnancy, and Mary spent the next three months. But we can well imagine the sharing that went on. It was all new for Elizabeth, though she was a few months ahead of her young cousin in the maternal experience. But Mary was the one of blessed faith, a faith Elizabeth's elderly husband had failed to bring her, and Mary's faith helped to make sense of Elizabeth's mysterious pregnancy.

If we give Mary a chance, not only will she bring Christ ever more fully into our lives with the joy of salvation, but also she will abide with us. She will be our life, our sweetness, and our hope. Mary will be with us as we face the vicissitudes and mysteries of life. If we have the ears to hear them, the words of the dying Christ still ring in our ears: "Behold your mother." Mary will come into our lives with her divine Son to the extent that we are open and ready to welcome them.

CALLING THE TWELVE

MARK 3:13–15

He went up the mountain and called to him those whom he
wanted, and they came to him. And he appointed twelve,
whom he also named apostles, to be with him, and to be sent
out to proclaim the message, and to have authority to cast
out demons.

Mark tells us, early in his narration of Jesus'
public ministry, that Jesus went up onto a
mountain and called those he wanted. God had
come into our midst in Christ so that we might find
our place in the midst of God. His descent into the
creation reached its depths when he stood in the
waters of the Jordan with the fish swimming about
him. As he rose up out of the waters and was con-
firmed by the Father's voice and the Spirit's descent
upon him, he began the homeward journey to Jerusalem, Calvary, resurrection, and ascension to the
Father's right hand.

So here he very symbolically goes up the
mountain. He has begun his ascent. And he calls
to this height, to this new level of consciousness,
those whom he wants. The throng, whom he has
come to save and will save, remain on the plain.
Many are called, few are chosen. His is the
freedom to call. What a grace it is to be called
by him.

The call does not usually come in the form of a tap on the shoulder. Rarely does he send an angel as he did to Mary of Nazareth, or even a saint as he did to Joan of Arc. The call more often comes in the form of a moment of insight in the midst of our musings—perhaps as we read words such as these, or through the sharing of a friend. We have to remain in listening mode, or we may well miss it.

He called those whom he wanted to call, and St. Mark tells us they came to him. The call respects our freedom. The response demands our freedom. It is up to us, when we hear the call, to come in response.

Those who were called, Mark goes on to tell us, were called to be with him and to be sent out. This at first sounds like a paradox. How can they do both?

I think this tells us that, first of all, we are to be with him. It is folly to try to be apostolic, to go out to help others, if we have not first connected with the Lord and become one with him. Conversely, the more we are with him, the more we are one with his life and mission—which is precisely to be sent out by the Father into this world for the salvation of all. So the more we are with him, the more we are sent out, however the apostolic love expresses itself in our particular vocation.

Even the most enclosed contemplatives, if they are one with Jesus, are fired with apostolic love, a love which, in their case, expresses itself through praying that the Lord send laborers into the fields, and through prayerfully supporting those laborers. Others go into the fields as one with Christ, to cast out the demons and bring the good news of salvation, to bring peace and joy in Christ through hope, whether through preaching and teaching or through the powerful witness of daily Christian life. Listen. Hear his call. Come to him. Be with him. And do whatever he tells you.

A NEW WAY OF LISTENING

LUKE 4:16–30

When he came to Nazareth, where he had been brought up, he went to the synagogue on the sabbath day, as was his custom. He stood up to read, and the scroll of the prophet Isaiah was given to him. He unrolled the scroll and found the place where it was written:

> "The Spirit of the Lord is upon me, because he has anointed me to bring good news to the poor. He has sent me to proclaim release to the captives and recovery of sight to the blind, to let the oppressed go free, to proclaim the year of the Lord's favor."

And he rolled up the scroll, gave it back to the attendant, and sat down. The eyes of all in the synagogue were fixed on him. Then he began to say to them, "Today this scripture has been fulfilled in your hearing." All spoke well of him and were amazed at the gracious words that came from his mouth. They said, "Is not this Joseph's son?" He said to them, "Doubtless you will quote to me this proverb, 'Doctor, cure yourself!' And you will say, 'Do here also in your home-town the things that we have heard you did at Capernaum.'" And he said, "Truly I tell you, no prophet is accepted in the prophet's hometown. But the truth is, there were many widows in Israel in the time of Elijah, when the heaven was shut up three years and six months, and there was a severe famine over all the land; yet Elijah was sent to none of them except to a widow at Zarephath in Sidon. There were also many lepers in Israel in the time of the prophet Elisha, and none of them *was cleansed except Naaman the Syrian." When they heard this, all in the synagogue were filled with rage. They got up, drove him out of the town, and led him to the brow of the hill on which their town was built, so that they might hurl him off the cliff. But he passed through the midst of them and went on his way.*

It was a great day for the backwater town of Nazareth. "Can anything good come out of Nazareth?"—that was the derisive saying making the rounds of the countryside. Well, today the hometown boy who has made good has come home, and he is going to show his stuff.

Then they will all see what can come out of Nazareth!

We each of us have our own way of listening. We are formed by all of our experiences to hear things in a certain way and to hear only certain things. The people of Nazareth listened in their own way that day, and they missed Jesus's meaning.

What Jesus said to the people of Nazareth was not new to them. They knew the Scriptures; that was almost all they ever read or heard. Yet their way of listening to Jesus was such that, when he reminded them of the widow of Zarephath and Naaman the leper, they were filled with indignation. They had their own way of listening to Jesus, and this is not what they wanted to hear from him.

The result: Not only were they upset, and not only did the meeting end in mob violence, but also

Jesus passed through their midst and walked away. They completely missed Jesus and his good news, because it did not fit into their way of listening.

Jesus walks into our daily lives in many ways— sometimes invited, sometimes not; sometimes welcome and sometimes not so welcome. But he always comes, the bearer of the good news. Yet how often do our pre-conceived notions, our way of listening, prevent us from hearing him? How often do we seek to harry him out of our lives, or at least out of a particular area of our lives, because his good news isn't the good news we want to hear? Do we want a God who skips to our tune, makes things work out the way we want them to work out? Perhaps many of us, if we are truly honest, will have to answer that question in the affirmative.

Maybe it is time that, instead of making Jesus and his good news fit into our usual way of listening, we let the divine wisdom open us out into a wholly new way of listening.

How? We can try stepping aside from our own concerns and looking at life from Jesus's perspective. It is a bit scary. It may do real violence to the way we have been listening up to now. But anyone who has really tried this can tell you it is the way to great joy and peace.

The Importance of Resurrection

MARK 12:18–27

Some Sadducees, who say there is no resurrection, came to him and asked him a question, saying, "Teacher, Moses wrote for us that 'if a man's brother dies, leaving a wife but no child, the man shall marry the widow and raise up children for his brother.' There were seven brothers; the first married and, when he died, left no children; and the second married her and died, leaving no children; and the third likewise; none of the seven left children. Last of all the woman herself died. In the resurrection whose wife will she be? For the seven had married her."

Jesus said to them, "Is not this the reason you are wrong, that you know neither the scriptures nor the power of God? For when they rise from the dead, they neither marry nor are given in marriage, but are like angels in heaven. And as for the dead being raised, have you not read in the book of Moses, in the story about the bush, how God said to him, 'I am the God of Abraham, the God of Isaac, and the God of Jacob'? He is God not of the dead, but of the living; you are quite wrong."

Mark's Gospel tells us that one day a group of Sadducees approached Jesus. In constant contention with the Pharisees, these men held that there was no resurrection. They were hoping to align Jesus with their position or at least trap him so that he could not accept the opposite. So they brought the fabricated story of a woman who successively married seven brothers and buried each of them. If there is a resurrection, whose wife is she?

I marvel at Jesus's patience. One group after another came at him, each making futile and rather stupid attempts to make him look bad. It was enough to try the patience of a saint, and maybe even that of this maker of saints, who deigned to be like us in all but sin.

In any case, on this particular occasion his answer was exceptionally forceful: "Is not this the reason you are wrong, that you know neither the Scriptures nor the power of God? . . . You are quite wrong." A literal translation of the Greek would yield an even more forceful response.

We might ask ourselves if Jesus might say of us also: "You are quite wrong." Is the way we are living our daily lives "quite wrong" because we do not understand the Scriptures or because we do not really believe in the power of God? Does the revelation of Jesus, given to us in the Gospels and Epistles, really lead and guide us in the way we live? Or are we following other, lesser lights that are not wholly informed by truth? Do we look to the Scriptures daily for guidance?

Here Jesus is pointing to the resurrection. St. Paul has told us: "If there is no resurrection of the dead, then Christ has not been raised; and if Christ has not been raised, then our proclamation has been in vain and your faith has been in vain. If Christ be not risen, then our faith is in vain" (1 Corinthians 15:13–14).

But the resurrection is not just an event that proves the authenticity of the Lord and his teaching. It is important that we keep our eyes on the risen Lord. Here we see the hope of our lives: We too shall rise.

This reality enlightens our days and helps us to keep things in perspective. In view of the eternal happiness that lies ahead for us, how great is the sorrow or pain of today, be it the pain of an hour, a week, a month, a decade, or many decades? What lies ahead for us is eternal, unending, everlasting— joy unlimited. "As it is written, 'What no eye has seen, nor ear heard, nor the human heart conceived, what God has prepared for those who love him'— these things God has revealed to us through the Spirit; for the Spirit searches everything, even the depths of God" (1 Corinthians 2:9–10). The risen Christ in glory at the right hand of the Father, the sight that filled the martyr Stephen with joy even as he was stoned to death, gives a whole new meaning to our lives.

But there is more. St. Paul has also reminded us that we who are baptized into Christ are to fill up what is wanting in the passion of Christ (see Colossians 1:24). Our sufferings united to those of Christ bring salvation and the joy of the resurrection to ourselves, our loved ones, and the whole needy world. This realization can turn pain and suffering into joy. What a privilege it is for us to be called to suffer redemptively with Christ. Not that suffering in itself is good. It is a consequence of sin and the abuse of nature. But it offers us an opportunity to grow in selfless and self-giving love. It is love that matters.

Keeping our eyes on the Risen One, we can go through our sufferings and everything else in this passing life with hope, joy, and expectation.

The Good Samaritan—
Out of the Box

Luke 10:25–37

Just then a lawyer stood up to test Jesus. "Teacher," he said, "what must I do to inherit eternal life?" He said to him, "What is written in the law? What do you read there?" He answered, "You shall love the Lord your God with all your heart, and with all your soul, and with all your strength, and with all your mind; and your neighbor as yourself." And he said to him, "You have given the right answer; do this, and you will live."

But wanting to justify himself, he asked Jesus, "And who is my neighbor?" Jesus replied, "A man was going down from Jerusalem to Jericho, and fell into the hands of robbers, who stripped him, beat him, and went away, leaving him half dead. Now by chance a priest was going down that road; and when he saw him, he passed by on the other side. So likewise a Levite, when he came to the place and saw him, passed by on the other side. But a Samaritan while traveling came near him; and when he saw him, he was moved with pity. He went to him and bandaged his wounds, having poured oil and wine on them. Then he put him on his own animal, brought him to an inn, and took care of him. The next day he took out two denarii, gave them to the innkeeper, and said, 'Take care of him; and when I come back, I will repay you whatever more you spend.' Which of these three, do you think, was a neighbor to the man who fell into the hands of the robbers?" He said, "The one who showed him mercy." Jesus said to him, "Go and do likewise."

Yes, they knew. Everybody knew. Those Samaritans, they were just plain bad. You could heap on them every negative adjective in your vocabulary, and you would still not be going too far. A Samaritan was a Samaritan, and that was that. End of discussion.

Then Jesus began his story. And they were caught up in it. They knew the road down to Jericho. They had gone that way many times, or they knew people who had made that journey. It was dangerous. Those brigands were something else. They would jump out on a solitary traveler and beat him for all he was worth. They would strip him bare, even taking his loincloth. There was just no mercy.

Yes, of course the priest passed by. What else could you expect from a priest? After all, he could not chance getting ritually unclean. And so, too, the Levite, the glorified altar boy. Then there was the Samaritan. He didn't have to worry about ritual uncleanness. He stepped in. He did what needed to be done: cleaned the wounds, bound them as best he could, loaded the man onto his donkey. . . .

Before they knew it, they were caught (I can just imagine Jesus smiling to himself: Gotcha!). Here was a Samaritan doing what was good, caring for a fellow human in his need—and a Jew at that. Their box was shattered. A good Samaritan!

We have perhaps heard the story too often. It is too well known to us to have its intended impact.

Moreover, "Samaritan" in no way carries for us the whole weight of centuries of animosity and prejudice. Perhaps we need to try something like the good Arab, or the good Jew, or the good gay, or the good fundamentalist, or the good panhandler. Or maybe even the good abortionist!

Actually Jesus never called the man the good Samaritan. That is our labeling. In fact he did not evaluate the person at all. He only asked: Who was a neighbor? He did not condone nor condemn Samaritan ignorance or error, prejudice, or atrocities. But charity covers a multitude of sins.

We all tend to put others in boxes. We may not be so blatant. We may not look down on a whole group (though the American superiority complex is well known among people in other countries). In our case it may be Uncle Fred, or cousin Lily, or the boss, or the local parish priest that we have boxed in. We know all about them. We know what to expect. We are glad we are not like them.

But who really is in the box? We think they are, but they go merrily on their way. And we are left in a box of our own making. It prevents us from ever discovering the beauty that God has created in those people. It prevents them from ever making the contribution to our lives that God intended our contact with them to bring to us. We are the prisoners of our prejudices, not the persons whom we seek to imprison in our narrowness and pride.

Let's trash all our boxes, and know the freedom of allowing every person to relate to us in all their beauty and giftedness. And let us not forget the word of our all-good Master: "Truly I tell you, just as you did it to one of the least of these who are members of my family, you did it to me" (Matthew 25:40). It is he, however deeply disguised, who comes to us in every human person.

NOT FAR—BUT NOT THERE YET

MARK 12:28-34

One of the scribes came near and heard them disputing . . . and seeing that Jesus answered them well, he asked Jesus, "Which commandment is the first of all?" Jesus answered, "The first is, 'Hear, O Israel: the Lord our God, the Lord is one; you shall love the Lord your God with all your heart, and with all your soul, and with all your mind, and with all your strength.' The second is this, 'You shall love your neighbor as yourself.' There is no other commandment greater than these." Then the scribe said to him, "You are right, Teacher; you have truly said that 'he is one, and besides him there is no other'; and 'to love him with all the heart, and with all the understanding, and with all the strength,' and 'to love one's neighbor as oneself,'—this is much more important than all whole burnt offerings and sacrifices." When Jesus saw that he answered wisely, he said to him, "You are not far from the kingdom of God." After that no one dared to ask him any question.

The Gospel lets us in on an interesting bit of dialogue.

A bright young fellow puts a question to Jesus: Which is the most important commandment?

Jesus responds, as we would all expect: First, to love the Lord your God with all your heart, soul, mind, and strength. Second, to love your neighbor as yourself.

With the cockiness of the young, the inquirer congratulates the Lord for his excellent answer, which he then rephrases.

It is Jesus' turn, and he benignly approves what the lad has had to say, adding: "You are not far from the kingdom of God."

"Not far"—but not quite there, either. For the bright young man's response was that which, in fact, most of us men—and I daresay some women also—give to the Lord's supreme command of love. Yes, love the Lord and neighbor "with all the heart" (in the Scriptures, the heart is the source of will-power), and "with all the understanding" (how we love to escape into the rational thing), and "with all the strength" (yes, our love should be proved in the doing).

But what has our typical male left out?

Jesus named four things. What about the soul— the feelings, the emotions, the source of tenderness and caring?

Alas, we have bought too much into the imaging of our culture, that macho image that we have been trying to export to the rest of the world (you can see the Marlboro man all over China these days). None of that mushy stuff for us!

Are we indeed lacking in soul? Are we afraid of it? Who is actually our model: Jesus or the Marlboro man or Schwarzenegger, or the Terminator, or another of that ilk? Maybe it is time we took a look. Didn't our Master, who was man enough to go unflinching to the cross, say to us: "Learn from me; for I am gentle and humble in heart" (Matthew 11:29)? Wasn't he a tender friend who could let one disciple rest his head upon his bosom, and accept a kiss from another? Yes, the customs of the times, of course, but bespeaking a tender, caring presence.

We haven't arrived at fulfilling the most important commandment, if we have not cultivated a tender, caring love for the Lord Jesus, for it is precisely in him that we find our God. Nor have we fulfilled it if we do not cultivate the same tender, caring love for our neighbors—our friends, our brothers and sisters, our colleagues, our companions on the journey toward the reign of God in our lives and in our world.

How far are we from the kingdom of God?

THE POWER OF THE BLOOD

MATTHEW 26:17–30

On the first day of Unleavened Bread the disciples came to Jesus, saying, "Where do you want us to make the preparations for you to eat the Passover?" He said, "Go into the city to a certain man, and say to him, 'The Teacher says, My time is near; I will keep the Passover at your house with my disciples.'" So the disciples did as Jesus had directed them, and they prepared the Passover meal.

When it was evening, he took his place with the twelve; and while they were eating, he said, "Truly I tell you, one of you will betray me." And they became greatly distressed and began to say to him one after another, "Surely not I, Lord?" He answered, "The one who has dipped his hand into the bowl with me will betray me. The Son of Man goes as it is written of him, but woe to that one by whom the Son of Man is betrayed! It would have been better for that one not to have been born." Judas, who betrayed him, said, "Surely not I, Rabbi?" He replied, "You have said so."

While they were eating, Jesus took . . . bread, and after blessing it he broke it, gave it to the disciples, and said, "Take, eat; this is my body." Then he took a cup, and after giving thanks he gave it to them, saying, "Drink from it, all of you; for this is my blood of the covenant, which is poured out for many for the forgiveness of sins. I tell you, I will never again drink of this fruit of the vine until that day when I drink it new with you in my Father's kingdom." When they had sung the hymn, they went out to the Mount of Olives.

The Passover is one of the most exciting stories of salvation history. It may be myth, that vehicle that bears truth too big for mere conceptual prose but rather resorts to the richness of poetry and tale. It tells us of the saving power of our God.

Moses, instructed by God, tells all the Hebrew people to gather in their homes. Each household is to slaughter a lamb, a perfect lamb, a lamb without blemish. Then the blood of the lamb is to be sprinkled on the doorposts of the house. All are to stay within, enjoy a feast of roast lamb, and get ready for a speedy departure. During the night the angel of the Lord swoops down on a terrible mission, finally to win the listening of a people and a ruler who ever closed their ears to the message of the Lord. The angel is to slay the firstborn son of each household. But wherever the angel sees the blood sprinkled upon the doorposts, the angel is to pass by.

Was it the blood of a dumb animal that saved the lives of rational animals, asks St. John Chrysostom? No! Rather, what did the angel see? The angel saw, not the blood of a lamb, but the blood of the Lamb of God. What was done in sacramental symbol that night in the Egypt of bondage is done in reality in the world where sin holds us all in bondage. It is the blood of the Lamb—the Lamb who is God's own Son—on our lips, the doorposts of the temple that we are, that saves us from the onslaughts of the angel who would now wreak havoc, the fallen angel, the evil spirit we call the devil or Satan.

This is the power of the blood. We drink the cup of salvation, the precious blood of the Lord, which poured forth from his side when he slept the sleep of death upon the cross, but which he had already given us in sacramental mystery the night before in the cup of the new covenant. Signed with this saving blood, we are safe.

The saving power of the blood will be sacramentally prefigured as Moses leads the redeemed people out through the Red Sea, our baptism; through the desert, our pilgrim journey through life; into the land of promise, the kingdom which has been promised to us. It is because we have been saved by the blood of the Lamb that we belong to the people of God and, led by our God-anointed leader, can confidently go forward knowing that the kingdom is our promised heritage.

Easter is a special time. The blood is fresh upon our lips. We go forward with the joy and enthusiasm of a new beginning, a vibrant hope. We vaguely know that the dog days of summer are ahead when we will have to plod along faithfully, struggling to keep our hope green. But for now, the risen Lord is very much with us. He has not yet ascended, going ahead to prepare the place for us. He walks at our side, opens the Scriptures for us, feeds us, challenges us, encourages us, prepares us for all that is to come. It is a good time. We know a oneness with him, for we have been bonded in his blood. We are more than blood brothers and sisters. We have all received his Spirit, and all together we cry out, with full confidence and love: Abba, Our Father.

This is the power of the blood. This is the joy of Easter.

AT THE LAST SUPPER

JOHN 16:21–27

When a woman is in labor, she has pain, because her hour has come. But when her child is born, she no longer remembers the anguish because of the joy of having brought a human being into the world.

So you have pain now; but I will see you again, and your hearts will rejoice, and no one will take your joy from you. On that day you will ask nothing of me. Very truly, I tell you, if you ask anything of the Father in my name, he will give it to you. Until now you have not asked for anything in my name. Ask and you will receive, so that your joy may be complete.

I have said these things to you in figures of speech. The hour is coming when I will no longer speak to you in fig-ures, but will tell you plainly of the Father. On that day you will ask in my name. I do not say to you that I will ask the Father on your behalf; for the Father himself loves you, because you have loved me and have believed that I came from God.

You have probably heard it, as have I: God never hears my prayers; he never answers—if there is a God. He said: "Ask and you will receive." But I ask and ask and never get anything.

I might answer with our Lord's little story of the pesky widow and the unjust judge (you can read the story in Luke 18:1–8). We do have to be persis-tent in our praying. But even then . . .

I think when we come to prayer we are sometimes like little children sitting on Santa's knee. We expect the benign Father to give us whatever we ask. We need to be childlike, but not childish. That is an important distinction. We see the shiny carving knife and want the immediate gratification of playing with it, in no way imagining what life without a finger or a hand might be like.

It might be better to see ourselves as mature children sitting down with our Father to look at things together and see what is best. Or, mindful of our Lord Jesus's words, "I have called you friends" (John 15:15), we might see ourselves as sitting with the Son, our friend. Before we ask for something, we need to take the time to see what we most want, and we need to consider whether the thing that looks gratifying to us at the moment is really conducive to that. As our wiser, more provident Father may see, what we are asking for now may, like the carving knife, lead to a real truncation, not only for a lifetime but for eternity.

Yes, ask and you will receive. But often it is not what we say we want but what we really want that God gives us: that which is conducive to our true and lasting happiness. Life on earth is immensely important. Every moment is precious and not to be squandered. But as important as our present life is, eternal life is infinitely more precious. God answers in the context of eternity.

God may seem to be saying no. He may even appear to turn a deaf ear. But in fact no prayer goes unheard or unanswered. We can take that on faith. And someone wiser than we is answering out of God's infinite wisdom.

On the night before he died, Jesus had a very special farewell meal with his chosen friends. In the course of that meal, the disciple who loved Jesus sat next to him, or rather in the fashion of that time, reclined next to Jesus so that he could lean back and rest his head on Jesus' chest and hear the beating of Jesus' heart. He hung onto every word Jesus spoke on that fateful night. And in later years, with the help of the Holy Spirit, he shared Jesus's words again and again until they were finally written down.

Among the words recorded are these: "I have said these things to you so that my joy may be in you, and that your joy may be complete" (John 15:11). All is to our joy—if we do it God's way.

And so, instinctively, while we ask for various things, we often add the proviso, as Jesus did in Gethsemane: ". . . yet, not my will but yours be done" (Luke 22:42). Father, do whatever you know is best for us. It seems to me that this is best for me right now, but you know. Your will be done—on earth as in heaven.

Ask and you will receive—whatever is for your true happiness and well-being, whether for yourself or for others. For the same infinite wisdom holds each of our dear ones, for each of whom we pray, in tender and caring love.

LOOK UPON HIM

JOHN 19:18–37

There they crucified him, and with him two others, one on either side, with Jesus between them. Pilate also had an inscription written and put on the cross. It read, "Jesus of Nazareth, the King of the Jews." Many of the Jews read this inscription, because the place where Jesus was crucified was near the city; and it was written in Hebrew, in Latin, and in Greek. Then the chief priests of the Jews said to Pilate, "Do not write, 'The King of the Jews,' but, 'This man said, I am King of the Jews.'" Pilate answered, "What I have written I have written." When the soldiers had crucified Jesus, they took his clothes and divided them into four parts, one for each soldier. They also took his tunic; now the tunic was seamless, woven in one piece from the top. So they said to one another, "Let us not tear it, but cast lots for it to see who will get it." This was to fulfill what the scripture says,

> *"They divided my clothes among themselves, and for*
> *my clothing they cast lots."*

And that is what the soldiers did.

Meanwhile, standing near the cross of Jesus were his mother, and his mother's sister, Mary the wife of Clopas, and Mary Magdalene. When Jesus saw his mother and the disciple whom he loved standing beside her, he said to his mother, "Woman, here is your son." Then he said to the disciple, "Here is your mother." And from that hour the disciple took her into his own home.

After this, when Jesus knew that all was now finished, he said (in order to fulfill the scripture), "I am thirsty." A jar full of sour wine was standing there. So they put a sponge full of the wine on a branch of hyssop and held it to his mouth. When Jesus had received the wine, he said, "It is finished." Then he bowed his head and gave up his spirit.

Since it was the day of Preparation, the Jews did not want the bodies left on the cross during the sabbath, especially because that sabbath was a day of great solemnity. So they asked Pilate to have the legs of the crucified men broken and the bodies removed. Then the soldiers came and broke the legs of the first and of the other who had been crucified with him. But when they came to Jesus and saw that he was already dead, they did not break his legs. Instead, one of the soldiers pierced his side with a spear, and at once blood and water came out. (He who saw this has testified so that you also may believe. His testimony is true, and he knows that he tells the truth.) These things occurred so that the scripture might be fulfilled, "None of his bones shall be broken." And again another passage of scripture says, "They will look on the one whom they have pierced."

The chosen people were on a journey, a long journey through the desert. They had sinned and sinned again, causing their journey to be prolonged. Now their sins brought among them poisonous serpents. The bite of these creatures meant death. The people cried out for healing. And an ever-compassionate God gave Moses the command: Fashion a bronze figure and raise it on a cross. All who look upon it will be healed. (The story is told in Numbers 21:4–9.)

Jesus is raised upon a cross above the city and outside its walls, for he is raised up not only for this city and these people, but for us all. Jesus is raised on high, and many look upon him. Pilate tried to determine what they should see: "The King of the Jews," his inscription read. But others had other eyes.

Some saw a hated rival, a threat to their power finally being overcome—so they thought—and they mocked and reviled him. Some saw a beloved in agony, and they agonized with him. One thief saw another beaten man and cursed all the more. But another thief saw something more and asked to go along on the journey into paradise. And it was an executioner, a pagan soldier, who cried out: "Truly this man was God's Son!" (Mark 15:39).

What do we see as we look upon him who has been pierced? Do we look with faith and hope and find healing? Do we really believe this is the Son of God, and that in his death is our life? As we struggle with the death-dealing wounds of sin, we need to look upon the one who has been raised up. There is no other salvation for us. He alone can save us from eternal death.

It is not enough for us to stand there with the sinless Virgin and experience something of the horror and pain of what is taking place. We are not sinless. We are deeply wounded by sin. And it is only if we look upon the crucified one, experience the price of our sin, and truly repent, that we can know the healing grace. The more we know the agony and pain our sins have caused and have demanded in their reparation, the more our looking upon this one who has been raised up is apt to be effective in our healing.

We have to be willing to acknowledge and expose our wounds to the healing balm that flows from the pierced hands and feet and side. We need humbly and gratefully to accept this healing, with a gratitude that impels us to seek to sin no more. Then our looking upon him who has been pierced will be for us a saving glance.

If we want to abide in our healed state, we need constantly to look upon him. The crucifix should not be just an ornament in our homes. It should be a constant invitation to an ever-deeper communion. He has been pierced for our offenses. In his wounds we are healed. Let us go forward in gratitude and in newness of life.

Perhaps our model here should be "the disciple whom [Jesus] loved." What enabled this young man to stay the course, when all the others had run? What made him worthy to hear: "Here is your mother"? What led him in all his writings to speak of himself as "the disciple whom he loved"?

Was it what he saw in those eyes, obscured though they were with blood, sweat, tears, and spittle? Even on Calvary, as he looked into those eyes, John had that ineffable experience of being the object of another's delight, of being truly accepted, embraced, and loved. Jesus had said: Seek and you will find. John had sought. And he found. He found love.

We, too, if we seek love in the face of the Beloved, will find love. Perhaps it is most easily found in the face of the Crucified. "No one has greater love than this, to lay down one's life for one's friends" (John 15:13). The experience will be ours if only we dare, with openness, to look upon him. To look into those eyes and let the love pour in. It scares us, of course—even though we long for it with our whole being. It scares us, because the only response to such love is love; we will have to give ourselves in return. But it is only in this communion of love that we will find all that we seek, as persons raised up to share divine life, joy, and being.

COME AND EAT

JOHN 21:1—14

*After these things Jesus showed himself again to the disciples
by the Sea of Tiberias; and he showed himself in this way.
Gathered there together were Simon Peter, Thomas called the
Twin, Nathanael of Cana in Galilee, the sons of Zebedee, and
two others of his disciples. Simon Peter said to them, "I am
going fishing." They said to him, "We will go with you."
They went out and got into the boat, but that night they
caught nothing.*

*Just after daybreak, Jesus stood on the beach; but the
disciples did not know that it was Jesus. Jesus said to them,
"Children, you have no fish, have you?" They answered
him, "No." He said to them, "Cast the net to the right side of
the boat, and you will find some." So they cast it, and now
they were not able to haul it in because there were so many
fish. That disciple whom Jesus loved said to Peter, "It is
the Lord!" When Simon Peter heard that it was the Lord, he
put on some clothes, for he was naked, and jumped into the
sea. But the other disciples came in the boat, dragging the net
full of fish, for they were not far from the land, only about a
hundred yards off.*

*When they had gone ashore, they saw a charcoal fire
there, with fish on it, and bread. Jesus said to them, "Bring
some of the fish that you have just caught." So Simon
Peter went aboard and hauled the net ashore, full of large
fish, a hundred fifty-three of them; and though there were
so many, the net was not torn. Jesus said to them, "Come*

and have breakfast." Now none of the disciples dared to ask him, "Who are you?" because they knew it was the Lord. Jesus came and took the bread and gave it to them, and did the same with the fish. This was now the third time that Jesus appeared to the disciples after he was raised from the dead.

Jesus had sent a message to the apostles that they were to go to Galilee and wait for him there. That made sense. Capernaum had become very much his home base, and it was hometown for a number of them. So off to Galilee they went. And waited. And got tired of waiting. Especially the ever up-and-at-'em Peter. "I am going fishing," he announced, and immediately they were all with him, out into the boat and out to sea.

It was one of those nights, though, when the fish seemed to have gone on holiday. Not a one came into their nets. At dawn's early light a rather discouraged crew looked toward the shore. It was time to go home—empty-handed. It didn't exactly help morale when a lone stranger (it was early and they had rather hoped to make it in without being seen) shouted across the waters: "You didn't catch any fish, did you?"

A possible customer he might have been, but they were not interested in customers right then. An unambiguous "No" was their reply. And then came the strange advice: "Cast your net on the other side."

Was there, deep down in them, some vague echo of another day when they had heard similar advice? Or was it simply that a dejected crew was ready to give it one more try?

Soon the net was not just holding; it was almost pulling the boat down. What a catch! It did not take long then to put two and two together. The "disciple whom Jesus loved"—and who loved him—knew: "It is the Lord!"

Again Peter was up-and-at-'em. He couldn't wait for the boat to pull in its great catch. He was already in the water and making for the shore.

And what did they find there? A charcoal fire and fish and bread slowly baking. Breakfast was on! This was the risen Lord, the one who had proved all his divine assertions without doubt, the Lord and Master. And yet he had gathered sticks, kindled a fire, and somehow found some fish and bread dough. He was fixing breakfast for his friends. Indeed, he himself served it, to each.

Things had not essentially changed. The divine was still a beggar for friendship. And, yes, there was that wonderful delicate touch: "Bring some of the fish that you have just caught."

Jesus has risen. He has ascended. He sits at the right hand of the Father. He is the glorified Lord of heaven and earth. And yet he is still with us, until the end of time. He promised. He is here as a friend, a serving friend. And—what I find more wonderful—he wants us to participate, bringing the gifts he has given us, in serving his friends. It is a wonderful community of mutuality, his circle. A most caring Lord invites us all to join in the care.

Come and eat! Jesus still says it: Come and eat me, come and eat the Eucharist, come and eat my word. But he doesn't stop there. He says it to all the poor and needy; indeed, he says it to all of us as he gives us our daily bread. He endows us with all the goods of his creating. And he invites each of us to contribute to the feast, bringing some of the abundance we have been able to gather with his help to help him feed his friends, especially those most in need.

A Christian is certainly one who follows Christ, accepts him as risen Lord and Master. And Christianity is built on friendship: Jesus calls us his friends. The Lord wants to share with us in a very human as well as divine way. An important part of that human sharing is our bringing to the gathering of friends a portion of what he has enabled us to have.

Come and eat! May the warmth, the caring, the tenderness of that day never be absent from our gathering about our risen Lord, who is ever in our midst.

About Paraclete Press
Who We Are

Paraclete Press is a publisher of books, recordings, and DVDs on Christian spirituality. Our publishing represents a full expression of Christian belief and practice—from Catholic to Evangelical, from Protestant to Orthodox.

We are the publishing arm of the Community of Jesus, an ecumenical monastic community in the Benedictine tradition. As such, we are uniquely positioned in the marketplace without connection to a large corporation and with informal relationships to many branches and denominations of faith.

What We Are Doing
Books

Paraclete publishes books that show the richness and depth of what it means to be Christian. Although Benedictine spirituality is at the heart of all that we do, we publish books that reflect the Christian experience across many cultures, time periods, and houses of worship. We publish books that nourish the vibrant life of the church and its people—books about spiritual practice, formation, history, ideas, and customs.

We have several different series, including the best-selling Paraclete Essentials and Paraclete Giants series of classic texts in contemporary English; A Voice from the Monastery—men and women monastics writing about living a spiritual life today; award-winning poetry; best-selling gift books for children on the occasions of baptism and first communion; and the Active Prayer Series that brings creativity and liveliness to any life of prayer.

Recordings

From Gregorian chant to contemporary American choral works, our music recordings celebrate sacred choral music through the centuries. Paraclete distributes the recordings of the internationally acclaimed choir Gloriæ Dei Cantores, praised for their "rapt and fathomless spiritual intensity" by *American Record Guide*, and the Gloriæ Dei Cantores Schola, which specializes in the study and performance of Gregorian chant. Paraclete is also the exclusive North American distributor of the recordings of the Monastic Choir of St. Peter's Abbey in Solesmes, France, long considered to be a leading authority on Gregorian chant.

DVDs

Our DVDs offer spiritual help, healing, and biblical guidance for life issues: grief and loss, marriage, forgiveness, anger management, facing death, and spiritual formation.

Learn more about us at our website:
www.paracletepress.com, or call us toll-free at 1-800-451-5006.

ALSO AVAILABLE IN THIS SERIES

PRAYING WITH MARY
Mary Ford-Grabowsky

80 pages   ISBN: 1-978-1-61261-137-2
$24.95 (pack of 5), Small paperback

PRAYING WITH ICONS
Linette Martin

64 pages   ISBN: 1-978-1-61261-058-0
$24.95 (pack of 5), Small paperback

PRAYING THE JESUS PRAYER
Frederica Mathewes-Green

64 pages   ISBN: 1-978-1-61261-059-7
$24.95 (pack of 5), Small paperback